Untamed Nostalgia

Wild Poems

By

Wafaa' Al-Natheema

ISBN: 1-4140-3808-9 (e-book)
ISBN: 1-4140-3807-0 (Paperback)

Library of Congress Control Number: 2003098980

This book is printed on acid free paper.

Printed in the United States of America
Bloomington, IN

1stBooks - rev. 04/15/04

In memory of my grandmother, Natheema A. Al-Faradhi, whose name I adopted as my family name.

To the souls of uncles Majid Salman and Khalid I. Hassoon.

Dedicated to my family and friends

Table of Contents

Introduction

I have been writing poetry and prose since the age of nine. I never published my Arabic poetry, but few of my English poems were published. Since 1990, my writing has mainly focused on non-fiction journalistic essays, reports and biographies, some of which have been published in newsletters and journals. However, writing poetry is a distinct departure from the many tasks and careers that I have undertaken: civil engineer, political scientist, teacher, translator, interpreter, radio host and producer, real estate salesperson, reporter and editor.

A variety of influential events have occurred in my life since the September 11 attacks that changed my perspectives of life and made me avoid work and people. Starting in May 2002, I began regularly writing poetry, memoirs and autobiography. I am in the process of publishing them.

"Untamed Nostalgia" is certainly a reflection of my feelings since a few hours after the onset of an illness in April 2002 and the aftermath of the "War on Terrorism". A majority of the poems are free verse with subjects varying from the deadly serious, pensive and philosophical, to true stories and whimsical or provocative themes.

I have arranged the poems loosely with no particular order and included one poem that I translated from Arabic. The three poems, "BUT," "Not A Recommended Mix," and "Untamed Nostalgia" were all written on September 24, 2003.

Read this book's poems with your favorite person, music and drink. Enjoy!

Wafaa' Al-Natheema
September 2003

From ZERO

So you think God chose you and only you to deliver God's message?
You think women are too weak to be prophets?
Incapable of keeping secrets,
Or preaching God's messages,
That God's words deserve for you to go to WAR,
That land and other possessions are worth killing for,
You think you are the only species that know it all?
You are stronger,
You are smarter,
You are wiser,
And everything on earth belongs to you;
Water, land, vegetation, animals, oil, air and women,
All are your possessions?

The science you contribute is to bring you privileges,
To bring you money, protection and conveniences,
Convenience; in that you make it serve you better.
Most of your clothes are made of cotton,
Most of women's clothes are not,
They are made from petroleum products.
They are exposing women as objects.
They are uncomfortable and limiting.
They are often insulting.
Women's clothes are unhealthy,
Are impractical and unworthy.

Eight out of ten contraceptives are made for women,
While MEN enjoy themselves,
with far fewer consequences.
Millions of MEN exploit, beat and/or rape women,
Everyday, everywhere …
What happens then? Nothing …
Your laws and religions protect you,
In return, you become the victims,
Women made you do the bad deeds, right?

Wafaa' Al-Natheema

And you are the angels,
God's chosen beings,
Everything you say goes,
Even when you rape or declare war on other nations?
You know it all?

You, leaders, told people to follow you,
Because you "knew it all"
Because yours was the "best way"
Directly or indirectly you've caused war and death.
You all assigned yourselves as leaders,
For others to follow your footsteps.
Males with testosterone,
You will continue to drive earth into death,
Unless women learn to boycott you.
Boycott your products,
Boycott your religions and politics,
Boycott working with and for you,
Boycott sleeping with you and giving you offspring.
Why do women go through pregnancy and delivery pain?
So that they deliver the infant to take after your family name?
Easily and readily made without any efforts,
Except for bed pleasures.
Children take your family name and not the women's,
So that yours keeps making history pages,
And women keep being the Unknown Soldiers,
Taken for granted.
It is time women unite in the boycott.
Woman does not come from man's rib,
Man comes from woman's womb.

May women gather to diffuse your power.
May on both sides women inject you with anesthesia,
Whenever you head to WAR,
So there will be no bloodshed, winners or losers.
May they place their arms around you,
Hug you and send you to Mama.

As Algerian women did,
In a successful bid,
Right after Algeria's Independence,
To prevent MEN from killing each other.
If a war is on,
May women, by the thousands, act as a shield,
By standing in the face of soldiers and make them yield,
To protect their sons, daughters and the field.
If women in such a vast number die,
MEN will suffer the ultimate pain.

Men, may you never see your loved ones.
May you end up alone and lonely.
May you see everything ugly.
You are dictators and unearthly.
No other creatures on earth are as narcissistic as MEN.
If you don't let women in the workplace or get equally paid,
If you want women only for your pleasure,
If you do not respect their opinion,
If you think their work is only in the household,
If you take advantage of them or take them for granted,
If you insist on dictating alone,
If you keep raping them and get away with it,
May women disappear from your life completely.
May forever you have no mates.
May you go mad and converse with yourselves.
May you end up doing it alone or with each other.
May you be left with animals,
To teach you better lessons,
To start from scratch,
From ZERO.

Zenobia

Arabian queen of renowned beauty
Defended the land fulfilling her duty
Was unyielding, intelligent, witty
She defeated a Roman Army
Meant to turn her country gloomy

Queen of Palmyra
A prosperous, yet a short era
The Romans returned to claim the land
To be under their full command
To turn it into a dim abode
In which they had their spoils bestowed
Taking Zenobia and her son prisoners.
Into Rome, the heart of winners.
Zenobia, in a blood line of victories and defeats
Her legacy is forever abiding in our hearts

To Write a Poem

I keep reading about poetry contests
The only time I won something,
was a seventy-five-dollar lottery ticket.
When I learned about the Grolier award,
I said, two hundred dollars?
That will pay one of my fifteen bills!
What about the other fourteen?
Do poetry contests on a monthly basis.
I sat crossing my legs in front of the TV
With a laptop, looking as if preparing a CV
Watching "Everybody Loves Raymond,"
Eating pastries stuffed with almond,
To get in the mood of writing my first poem!
Commercials! are indeed a "great incentive"
TV's music, dizzying action and Ads are so "exciting!"
The time was approaching midnight.
Feeling tired while thinking of calling home,
I turned the TV off, what a noise!
During a tranquil time, I heard the snoring of my cat
It was a very soft snoring unlike human's
A lullaby like, it soothes and smoothens.
After writing the above,
I know now I can provide instructions,
How to write poetry!
The first is to have a laptop,
The second is to put the top on your lap,
Concentrate, breathe and don't gasp
Sit in front of the TV.
Then describe your environment,
And a poem will be born.
It is just that it won't win any contests!

Wafaa' Al-Natheema

Promotion via Poetry

Have you read a poetry book before,
That has taken you to shore after shore?
From India to Russia and America,
From the Arab World into Africa,
Roaming between dreams and reality,
Riding through humor and calamity?

"Untamed Nostalgia" is inclusive of romance,
War, peace, food, music and dance,
Philosophy, TV and family members,
It teases the mind and so one remembers,
It mentions events of high importance,
Narrates history of great significance.

"Untamed Nostalgia" is for,
Animal, women and political activists
History lovers and food specialists
Poets, music lovers and optimists

Daring, provocative and enhancing the self
Hurry to obtain a copy from top of a shelf.
The poet is confident, not full of conceit
The book will affect even those with cold feet!

This poem gives an idea for promotion using poetry.

6

Had it Not Been For You

I cannot tell you how much I've been missing you,
I even copied your laughter in some of my life episodes,
That loud and cute laughter—childish and innocent.

Youngest uncle, my beloved,
I long for those playing days,
Joking even about the little insects and lizards!

That story you once told me,
You fainted when you saw your own blood.
I suffocate every time I imagine you in war,
That foolish Iran-Iraq War.
I close my eyes with a sigh,
When the thought passes my mind.
In a blood bath, in a killing field with insanity.
How did you tolerate it, my dear?
What an agony you must have felt,
when you were shot and killed.
Or are you still a war prisoner?
Till when I tarry in hope,
Wondering in my thought loop,
Whether or not you are returning home.

Had it not been for your laughter,
Had it not been for your innocence,
Had you not told me about fainting from blood,
I would have declared a complete boycott against men.
I am already constantly challenging them.
My dear, sweet Ammo*:
I know you are riding the tranquility stallion,
Away from our world's pain,
Into the world of the divine.
To you, Majid Selman
I dedicate this poem.

May through it,
Your name and your legacy become global,
And everything you've touched turn noble.

*Uncle
Majid Selman disappeared one month before the end of the Iran-Iraq war. He is the poet's uncle (on her father's side). They both had fond memories during the poet's childhood and teenage years.

May You Rest In Peace

Tonight is Friday, June 14th, 2002   I was watching twenty/twenty
You may have watched it too   with Carol Burnett, funny and witty
Her daughter passed away due to   lung cancer at eight and thirty
My uncle had lung cancer too   he departed at age two and fifty
Both heavy smokers, those two   were young and full of activity
My mind delivered impromptu   I'd never seen it in such lucidity
Carol is funny and uncle too   both were acting before twenty
My improvisation, like a Mulatto   black and white, clear and misty
With my thought, as if in a grotto   spacing in and out, felt hoity-toity
Uncle left acting and traveled to   Russia for architecture, what a pity

He was so humorous spitting jokes   making people tear from laughter
In Russia, he was young and active   a talented architect and dancer
When he returned to Iraq single   uncle only worked in architecture
He married a woman he knew   nothing about, what a disaster
She gave birth to Nadia and Zaid   they were unhappy with each other
Uncle and wife were miserable   I often see them argue when together
Zaid is now a genius in computer   Nadia graduated and became mother
Zaid completed his Master's   ranked Iraq's first with honor
Uncle would have been so proud   but he passed away from cancer
On Thursday, September 28th   1989 in Boston, Gone forever

I remembered uncle saying "shto"   while half awake in Mass hospital
"Shto," "Spasiba," "Pazhalisto"   Russian in an American hospital

Wafaa' Al-Natheema

Surprised, I laughed joyously
Give him kisses and a big hug
But the cancer was spreading
Praying, being angry, crying
We came back with instructions
I was numb, exhausted and sad
At home, I tried to comfort him
His mind despite cancer attack

he was cute, I wished to cuddle
at that time he felt better in general
mushrooming, mean, not genial
nothing changes the status of uncle
medications hoping to be merciful
I never witnessed something as awful
alone while working, was incredible
was so sharp, detailed and capable

His humor didn't trend away
His details, examples, stories
I remember he loved cream
Every time we drank cream
Shocking but true, he smoked
He neither quit nor apologized
Everyday for two months, I
I tried my best to comfort him
Doing that made me so numb
When he departed, it was as

his history knowledge was so intact
dates and names, were all exact
so did I, we often drank it together
people commented, we didn't bother
till he lost consciousness in bed
as Carol Burnett's daughter did
managed his medicine and food
kept him busy, in a good mood
but got me very attached to him
though the world became so dim

Hurt for long, I couldn't weep
His ring, I decided to keep

a tearless agony that was so deep
his belongings were taken home

He came to the states alive
I did continuously strive

but thin, faded, did not survive
to make him feel as if at home

I needed help, I asked mother   to come to the US and be together

She, myself, uncle and father   but they were both so insensitive

A wonderful, idealistic MAN   was at their mercy and poor plan

Of their arguing, I was not a fan   so I began to take the initiative

When once we were at a dispute   so intense, uncle cried, destitute

Seeing his tears made me execute   a reproach on my parents' morale

His departure left a scar in me   he is in my thoughts, invaluable

His name, K. H. A. L. I. D.   is Khalid: Arabic for immortal

* The poem was completed on August 16, 2002. It is comprised of fifty-two lines (Arabic-style) to symbolize the age of the poet's uncle who passed away. Khalid I. Hassoon is the poet's uncle on her mother's side. The last twelve lines are spaced purposely.

*Beebee**

The forgotten martyr …
Married at age fourteen
Her years of marriage were fifteen
She gave birth to five:
Two died young, three were to survive.
Before her departure, only two were alive
Her eldest son deceased with cancer
Her youngest daughter,
Never saw her father.
She was a widow before thirty
Poor with a burden, so hefty
Natheema*, the forgotten martyr.

When her two children passed away
People blamed her, chained her with guilt and dismay
Her fate and flock have gone astray
Yet her husband has no duty or a say!
Bed pleasures with food readily offered on a tray!

Then her youngest daughter,
An orphan,
Married young at fifteen,
To a first cousin, her senior by fifteen.
Marriage was to bring her "freedom"
Was to provide her a better home.

Natheema protested: "The marriage is wrong"
"His mother was mean to me, I was not strong"
"His mother beat me, life was not a happy song"
But the orphan daughter insisted
On herself, a gloomy fate inflicted

Natheema lived with son-in-law and daughter
Like a nanny raising their son and daughter
Cooking and cleaning,
With no respect or a kind heart,
With no appreciation, fight after a fight.

Her family was so mean and lofty,
Filling her life with morbidity,
With tears, pain and travesty.
Beebee: My life with you was short and hasty,
I long for you, your stories and food, so tasty.
Farewell, martyr.
May you rest in peace.

* Beebee is the term used to call grandmothers in Iraq. Natheema is the name of the poet's grandmother (on her mother's side). She passed away on February 16, 1997.

She Called at Five Thirty in The Morning

Within half an hour,
Memories of three trips to Iraq came to mind.
Within half an hour from her majesty's call,
I began to remember them all.

Every time I travel there,
I return in debt with no work.
I even got very sick
On one of those trips.
What an omen!
I took gifts,
That left nothing in my bank accounts.
Gifts to all uncles and cousins,
Who never ask about me!

Not one of them has sent me a letter,
Not one has called to make me feel better.
All these years while in Diaspora, not one.
Even those with generous gifts: None.
The only two letters I've ever received,
Were to ask me favors from cousin Ahmed.

On my second trip, I took an expensive gift,
To teach Zaineb a skill would be a shift,
From being home and domestic cleaning,
A skill that would allow her to earn a living,
And improve her life with some meaning.
I gave her a pricey kit to learn weaving,
Zaineb was not enthusiastic about learning.

Last night, I made a mistake,
I called my uncle, her father.
I informed him of a family friend whose daughter
Has been suffering from cancer.

Then I received a call six hours later,
Waking me up from sleep at 5:30 A.M.
On a Sunday to ask me for a favor.
Zaineb it was, requesting money,
Instead of saying "I miss you honey!"
They own a home.
But she wants a bigger one
In the middle of embargo, bombs and calamity!

The first time she ever called and only.
I don't just give them gifts, I call them quarterly.
Who will support me when I am lonely?
Who will come to my rescue when in need?
Definitely not she or uncle.
I shall save every nickel.

Two Friends

One reads stories
The other listens and criticizes
They tease one another
Everybody laughs
The reader is alone and lonely
His family? In the Diaspora:
Two in the UK,
One in the US of A
The listener's family joins in listening,
Gives opinions that are strengthening,
Or throws in jokes, then laughing.
Two friends for years,
They lived in fears,
One war after another,
Yet they stayed together.
Connected through memories and friendship
Not work, blood or religious worship
Relaxing, reading, following their bliss
Focusing, making sure nothing to miss
Unhappy when times pass.
Then the reader leaves home,
To join his family,
Hoping not to be alone or lonely.
He learns of his friend, the listener,
That his daughter has cancer,
Living with her husband, son and daughter.

In the Diaspora
What an era!
The listener stays behind
With too much in mind
Four months later, he heads to bed
Never wakes up, leaves a dread.

16

Clever

His Arabic name means clever
Never have I seen one like him ever
The epitome of patience
Calm with alive conscience
His grimace is apt to grin
Smiles are wide, from within
Clever does not wither in groove
Needs not shift gears or move
Somehow time passes and he'd improve

So patient and able
Aidant, generous and noble
Reads stories, philosophy and poetry,
Featuring wisdom, humor and victory.
Not physically handsome, he doesn't worry.
He is not ardent yet zealous
It takes him a while to be jealous
He is clever: A name fitting the named
Handy to befriend, naturally tamed

*Ghazala and Nimir**

The Love of my life …
My unconditional lovers,
Unlike human lovers.

It was a mystery: Whenever I sang,
They'd come and cuddle,
They'd hug and form a bundle,
Hugging, embracing, licking and kissing,
Every time they heard my singing!

What precious beings,
I enjoy their doings.
So playful and innovative
They make one appreciative
Compared to them, humans are indeed behind,
In showing emotions and freedom of mind.

Ghazala likes to massage my neck
Nimir tosses on my tummy and back
The love of my life filling me with grace
I enjoy them nibbling in my face.

When Nimir departed, she left a dreadful scar,
In my conscience with memories from afar.
I hear her from the realms above
From paradise of celestial love!

---

* Ghazala and Nimir are the poet's two female cats. Nimir passed away on
July 23, 2002, from cancer and had bled for two months. Ghazala, her sister,
has also been diagnosed with cancer and began bleeding in September 2003.

American Cuisine

Better not eat at all
Everything is bad for you:
Red meat, fat, oil, coffee, eggs,
Sugar, salt, soda, pastries
Don't eat quickly.
Chew your food, or else.
Don't eat and sleep immediately.
Don't think or read while eating.
Have positive thoughts, or get sick.
Eat small meals and don't snack.
Exercise … Emphasize …
Drink lots of water;
If less than eight glasses a day,
You'll end up in hell.
Come to think of it, water is useful in hell,
It cools off the heat.
Eat lots of fiber, or your "you know what" gets stuck
Layered cheese pizza with chips and diet coke,
Eggs, buttered toast and bacon with skim milk,
Are examples of taking it easy with calories!
Or dieting!
Better eat nothing.
Gather my friends, I invite you to dinner.
Gourmet American Cuisine:
Spring WATER, ORGANIC folic acid,
MULTI-VITAMIN Stew,
And plenty of tofu.

Wafaa' Al-Natheema

Sushi

Layers of ecstasy …
Wrapped in delicacy …
The epitome of art
Delicious, tasty, smart

The inventor was a scientist
With features of an artist

Exotic raw fish makes the mouth water
Healthy, ideal for defeating cancer
With rice to quench one's hunger,
Wasabi*: To turn the body into a dancer,
Zesty, peppery, a great enhancer.
Shifting from a taste to another via ginger.

Are you still fishy?
Then taste Sushi

* Green mustard.

The Love Poet
*by Lamee'a Abbas Amara**
Translated from Arabic by Wafaa' Al-Natheema

Alone on the Atlantic shores,
Only your memory exhilarates me,
In my room …
Pardon me; it is not my room,
It is my jail.
Through the window, I watch the living,
Filling the sunny shore.
A festival for every couple,
Like a stallion, disobedient, willful,
With attire so little.
From my room,
I talk of love,
And of passion that I never felt,
As a philosopher
Describes the liquor,
Which he never drank.

* Lamee'a Abbas Amara is a renowned Iraqi poet currently living in San Diego.
Al-Natheema has won the Der-Hovanessian Translation Award of the New
England Poetry Club in November 2002 for translating this poem.

L.O.V.E.

L.O.V.E.
If I don't write about it,
They would not consider me a poet,
They'll think I am a weird woman.
A Sort of annoying rule.

L.O.V.E.
Attacked me at age nine!
Was one-sided affair with tears.
Lasted long, five years.
He was same as my age,
Son of a rich with no courage.

L.O.V.E.
A feeling I had until I was twenty-five
Too many years,
Of pain and tears.
At that age, I began to like,
And make friends only.
No more pain and feeling lonely.
At age twenty-five,
I kissed L.O.V.E. good-by.
Since then, I have been experiencing good omens.
At twenty-six, graduated from engineering.
At twenty-seven, bought a condo and owned a business.

At thirty, I incorporated my business,
Started a newsletter, then graduated from political science.
At thirty-four, I founded a non-profit organization.
I have been sinking in an ocean of accomplishments.
Do you blame me for kissing L.O.V.E. good-by?

Dililloul

Dililloul, Oh my son, dililloul
May your enemy suffer and live forever alone
Dililloul, my daughter, dililloul
May your wisdom thrive to succeed the throne
Dililloul, my grandmother, dililloul
I am in so much pain since you've passed away
I missed you, come to my thought every day
Dililloul, lie beside me grandma, and fall asleep
The best storyteller I've known, I wish to weep
Dililloul, you made me cry and laugh
You narrated your life, was so tough
Dililloul, my father and my mother
I wish to see you respect each other
I missed the old times being together
With uncles and sweet grandmother
Dililloul, Oh diaspora, what a curse you are
May no one feel you and may you go far
Dililloul, children, women and men
May you be forever protected, Amen

* Dililloul is the title of a popular Iraqi lullaby. It is a meaningless word for
chanting purposes. The first two lines are taken directly from the famous lullaby,
which has been chanted to children for over a century, and later became a
well-known Iraqi song. The poet hopes to compose and sing it.

Indian Music

They have not invented yet,
an expression for "Beyond Spirituality"
It is Indian Classical Music,
When ecstasy is quick,
Magnetizing consciences like gravity.

Music with violent cognizance,
With oceanic waves of senses,
Radically awakens, gently relaxes.

Taste the "Beyond Spirituality,"
Listen to Indian music.
Substitute your anti-depressant medicine
With Indian music, begin envision.
Rid yourself of body ache,
With yoga and Indian music.

People of earth, I am possessed,
I am addicted, I've confessed.
Ta De Ta ...... Tateta De
Takeka Da ...... Da ... Da
Formulas for spiritual intoxication.
They highly challenge the imagination,
A Kama Sutra for the mind and soul.
Raging with no control.
Beyond Spirituality!

Holy Land

You are probably thinking Jerusalem, Bethlehem or Mecca.
They are all holy lands,
But not as holy as the opulent land of poetry,
Oceanic contributions and an ancient history.
Bethlehem, Jerusalem and Mecca,
Did not produce well-noted scientists, engineers and doctors.
The world did not come to them to acquire knowledge.
The Holy Land I mean is unique.
Her offspring are various civilizations.
The only land that gave birth to more than two civilizations,
Gave birth to five.

The land of Greeks, Japanese, British, Romans,
Turks, Spaniards, French and Germans,
Gave birth to one.
The land of Egyptians, Indians, Persians,
Chinese and Russians,
Gave birth to two.
The Arabs gave birth to two; ancient and medieval.

In America, the European Christians,
Are having their first birth.
Those who confiscated a land by force and terrorism,
Claiming that God promised them the land,
Think they are contributing,
And giving birth to a civilization!

Theirs are forcefully carved out homes, waters and streets,
Made possible by yearly US generous grants!

The Holy Land I am flirting with,
Has contributed to civilization five times.
The Sumerians rose, then fell.

That is ONE
Then Babylonians came,
That is Two
Followed by Assyrians,
Three
Then the Akkadians,
Four
Last, but not least, the Arab Muslims,
That is FIVE.

I challenge you to name other lands,
That gave birth as many times.
Abraham lived there.
Laws were invented there.
Not to mention the treasures of oil,
Engulfed by rivers and fertile soil.
There, the offspring of six thousand years.
The land's name denotes its reality,
Deeply rooted and original
*I*ncomprehensible
*R*espectable
*A*ccountable
*Q*uintessential

From Africa to America

People are so diverse ethnically,
Yet they behave similarly.
They point the finger at each other,
Having flourishing empires that wither,
With same conducts, enslaving one another.
They all prominently enslaved Africans:
Asians, Australians, Europeans and Americans.
Even Africans sold Africans!
What an awful practice and a norm,
Lacking piety and a just form.

Enslaving based on the skin and hair
The darker the skin, the fewer things to share
The fewer the privileges, better not dare
It is scary how much one can bear

All slaves came from Africa
Shackled in chains to America.
How they coped and contributed,
Is worth being documented!

Ancient Bride

No one knows how ancient she is.
Beyond ancient, yet still thriving.
History knows how long she has been suffering.
How many times they have tried to kill her.
But she and the mercury behave alike,
No one can spot or contain her.
With seven souls,
Great determination,
And oceanic contribution.
Ancient, yet thriving,
Unconditionally loving.
Everyone wants to lay a finger on her,
To see how it feels to tamper with her,
To tease or hurt her,
To test her endurance,
To undermine her importance.
Everyone is jealous of who she is,
And of what she possesses.
Eat your heart enemies,
She does not react,
She will act,
And stay intact.
She does NOT quit,
A marvelous princess,
Unique among princesses and queens.
A bride, not any bride.
Baghdad, the Ancient Bride.

The Price of Peace

There is no hope for peace,
Unless women boycott men.
As mothers, sisters or wives,
They should hug men around them,
And send them home.
To avoid wars and bloodshed,
As Algerian women did,
In a successful bid,
To prevent men from killing themselves,
Right after Algeria's independence.
Sadly, the HIStorians did not document its details,
Events are not important when achieved by females.
If hugging and persuading men does not help,
And a war is approaching,
There will be no hope,
But for women to boycott men.
To boycott their products,
their religions and laws.
To boycott sleeping with them,
And giving them offspring.
To protest men's actions and foolishness,
To fast from talking with them.
If war is on,
There will be no hope to stop it unless,
Women, by the thousands, act as a shield,
Facing soldiers and forcing them to yield,
To protect the lives of people and the field.
May women inject testosterone carriers,
With anesthesia, every time they head to war,
So there will be no winners or losers,
No lives lost, only peace with lovers.
I am not a dreamer,
I am a strong believer.

Cartoons, Classical Music and Literature

Superb Cartoons …
Glorious Tunes …
Great Literature …
Wonderful Architecture …

Sadly, I've never seen her
My uncles and father did
And everybody said;
All that about Russia.
I've grown up watching Russian cartoons
Some of my principles came from these films and tunes
Emotionally touched by their music and ballet
Wondering will I ever roam in a garden or a chalet,
Dance the Kazachik*,
Listen to classical music,
Learn the musical language,
Read and appreciate Russian literature,
Absorb the wonderful architecture?

Regretting not seeing her before Perestroika.
I would have been able to compare,
Analyze, comprehend and declare,
What may not be foretold in a story or a song,
The truth may die upon the tongue,
In the propaganda of the winner and strong,
Like a vacillating music.

Glorious Russians:
From Dostoevsky
To Tchaikovsky
Composers of the greatest classical music
Writers of the best literature
Creators of deconstructivist^ architecture
Founders of giving birth under water

Winners of endless Olympic medals
They lost it all in wars and aggression
In rigid dictatorship and oppression
In bowing hastily to capitalism
Not taking the middle road away from communism.

* A Russian dance, transliterated so to fit the rhyme.
^ The term is used for a special type of modern architecture.

Muffins, Jazz and Technology

The best muffins …
Embracing raisins …
Or hugging blueberries and other stuffing
Soft, cushiony, with cinnamon filling
A magical taste with a cup of tea
Felt at home, at work or near sea
Hunger filling …
Desire fulfilling …
I let you melt in my mouth, then I sing
Instantly my soul gives birth to a wing

Muffins in the country of Jazz
Colorful luxury; red and turquoise
Jazz: The innovative improvisation
Harmonizing the mind with imagination
Influenced by Arabic tunes
Brought in via Muslim Africans

Jazz in the country of technology
Leading the world in every -logy
With absolute power and might
Making her wisdom depart
Inflicting the world with fright
What a pity!

From her glorious fifties
To the war era of the sixties
Since then, she never ceased wars
On all fronts: Air, lands and shores
Becoming utterly covetous
Despite being more than copious

The country of muffins, jazz and technology
Owes the world tons of apology
I hope she comes to her senses
Begins by paying attention to consensus:
That people do not want war!
It is time to be acknowledged by those in power.

Wafaa' Al-Natheema

Here and There

Here, they send flowers for the dead,
There, they send lamb and other food.
Here, they dress and make up the dead,
There, they cover hiv* with cloth in wood.
Here, they have a party and gifts before giving birth,
There, they wait forty days after giving birth.
To make sure the baby is healthy and will survive.
One adopts "the written," the other wants to thrive.
Planning ahead as they do here,
Is a funny habit over there,
How can they plan ahead,
When matters are written everywhere?
Pre-written by the divine, fate or nature.
They can schedule themselves for next week or month,
But not for longer, affected by destiny, wars and death.
Here, they play football with hands,
There, football is played without hands,
Or it is a foul.
Here, they make love,
There, they feel love,
It is hilarious to make it.
Here, they have sex before marriage,
There, they do after.
Here, they put the month before the day,
There, and everywhere else, the month comes after.
Here and there are foreign,
So foreign, we need interpreters,
Diplomats, passports and visas.

* Neutral (third-person) pronoun used by the poet.

34

Freedom

That who looks for freedom,
Is as if seeks slavery.
Its presence is as the soul's,
As that of the conscience.

That who seeks something,
Is as if it is absent.
Freedom is not absent.
Inhaling its fragrance is natural.
Freedom is intangible.

Its presence is as the oxygen we breathe,
As the skies and clouds we live beneath.
Freedom is spiritual
Feeling it is sensational

Though humans versified codes and rules,
And created religions and laws,
They often break them.
They hide free behind the slavery fence,
As if shackled demanding freedom's presence!

Pensive Mind—Thoughts to Bind

On Death's domain, I carefully listen and fix my eyes,
Where human nature is in test between truths and lies.
With meditative mind, I search the gloomy abode,
In which the conqueror has his spoils bestowed.
Whole kingdoms in the subjugator's den use thrust,
While nations follow and are weakened like dust.
Why is power bowed to and lingers for so many years,
Until a violent coup by someone suddenly appears?
Quenchless, the conqueror gluts the vast tomb
So mighty, yet acts primitively as if in the womb
Greed, lust and terror are continuously spread,
Filling humans with war of mind and dread.
Thousands of bodies, killed in the field
Still obstinate, imprudent, never yield
Even dignity has been compromised and laid aside
Mourning has not ceased and tears have not dried
Those who lost loved ones, they vivify in stages
The drama of their lives can fill many book pages
With those universal thoughts, humans bind
Forcing us to analyze, enhancing the pensive mind

*Learn to Eat Problems for Breakfast**

It is rare for people to seek challenge.
Many lack endurance and courage.
Common are those who seek facile tasks and shortcuts.
People run away from struggle and agony,
Lest they collapse.
Yet pain and struggle are life's real tastes.

Effortless wishes bring evanescent happiness.
Uttermost long-lived aroma of gladness,
Is inhaled when overcoming and tolerating pain.

So learn to eat problems for breakfast;
For to feel joy, is to be prepared to face them.

* Title anonymous

BUT

I thought I would rise in love again,
BUT I am getting older and older.
My principles have been the same,
BUT my heart and energy have not.
What should I do if I look younger,
And men are deceived?
I am getting older only in age,
BUT not physically and spiritually!
I don't think I can handle love now
At forty-three,
I am still free,
BUT lonely
Marriage? What an institution!
Men think I am independent
Don't qualify for this holy institution!
They want a dependent woman,
So they feel needed and superior
BUT then complain: She is a burden!
Men don't know what they want,
BUT women do.
Sometimes, they become uncertain.
BUT only when accompanied by men.

The Positive Prescription

When you are poetic,
You feel zoetic*
If you can't be one,
Then become enthusiastic.
When unable to achieve this,
Get physical and be energetic.

If you still feel pessimistic,
And matters seem problematic,
Stay in the cellar, not in the attic.
"If you hit bottom, there is no way but up"^
So cheers and chin up.

* Zesty
^ Arabic proverb.

Short Thoughts

Religions

Islam is to surrender to the will of one God
The Creator
Otherwise, surrender to the will of Mother Nature
If you believe there is no Creator
Or submit to your mind power
And fulfill your Buddhist or Taoist desire

It is most puzzling:
Religions were born to mean well
Yet in practice, they turn our lives to hell
Conflicts of all colors
Drum-beating wars
Three major monotheistic religions
Believing in one God, not several gods
Yet they interpret God variably
Then provoke each other severely!

***

Traffic Lights

Red … Yellow … Green
Are important to be seen

One day, a thought came to mind:
What happens if many were colorblind?

40

Candles

In the East:
Candles melt away to bring lights
For rituals, prayers and joy of hearts

In the West:
Candles burn for beauty and romance
Scented, flicker with music and dance!

***

Red Wine

A controversial drink!
Before the discovery of ink
Nations forbade it
Others allowed it

Here is the dilemma:
Its acidity upsets many stomachs
Yet medicine encourages it for the hearts!
Why not inject wine directly to the hearts?
Is it a true finding?
Or are wine businesses profiting?

***

Let's Yoga

Wide open your legs
Suck in your belly
Breathe in, breathe out
Again inhale, exhale
Just practice it quietly
Sleeping will be heavenly.

***

Her Teeth and the Mongol Invasion*

She was giving a workshop
I perplexed by her teeth
Why were they light purple,
If her lipstick was red?
Where was the missing blue?
Purple! The color of the Tigris
From ink and blood
When the Mongols invaded Baghdad.
Why were her teeth so purplish?
My mind, embarrassingly larkish:
Aha, blue from smoking!
Had she not combined the two
I would have listened and learned too!

***

Palm Pilot*

She knew I was an Arab
Immediately after the September attacks,
While I was spaced out, she asked:
"Are you familiar with palm pilot?"
From swimming in my thoughts,
I strove back to answer her:
"No, I am not a pilot, God forbid,
I am a civil engineer!"

*True story   Palm Pilot is an electronic organizer.

Anti-Routine and Clichés

Bathe in the lake
Buy everything fake
Urinate on the plants
Don't go to work
Let the dog bark
Don't bother washing every morning
Why use a hair dryer,
When the sun is hotter?
Do work while walking.
Interrupt when people are talking.
Anything you've been doing regularly
Stop!

***

Strange "L" Words

Fascinating!
Life complicating …
Lalapalooza means "dilly" or "daisy"
Lampoonery means "satire" or "raillery"
According to the dictionary:
"Larruping" means "very"
Next time, for a change, say:
Lalapalooza & Lampoonery are larruping contradicting
Just make sure you carry your passport with you!

***

Exhaustion

Why do people reach exhaustion,
When the body gives us signs?
Unless all are mentally challenged,
There is no other explanation!

Krishna

A musician …
A cowherd …
Everybody's friend
A will that doesn't bend
Yet humble …
And so gentle …

***

I Am So Rich!

Today, there were five hundred dollars,
In my bank account, pearls and flowers.
After all checks have been deducted,
I still have some extra!
This is a wonderful era.
I've developed a complex though:
"Insufficient Funds"

***

Only Humanity

Can the human mind conceive of it?
Can humans become it?
A new century where there is
No ethnicity …

No nationality …
Only humanity.
Yes, in the month that has no Friday!

***

Chinese

What does it mean,
When a language is so tough to learn?
Its speakers are complicated,
Or sophisticated?

***

An Old Indian Wisdom

To acquire wealth,
You need to first seek knowledge
The longer the knowledge bond with Saraswathi*
The more jealous Lakshmi* becomes
And wealth will shower you forever!

* Saraswathi is the goddess of knowledge. Lakshmi is the goddess of wealth.

***

Earth

She is made of soil
Of air and water
For all to share
Lavish and ethereal space
Breezes nibble her face.
Humans filled her with Uranium
And products of Petroleum!

***

45

Lao Tzu

"True goodness is like water.
Water gives life to ten thousand things,
But does not compete with them"

Spiritual words, wisdom filling
Individuality and ego killing
Tao Te Ching is challenging
To human being

***

Fortune Cookies

Ten years ago, I kept one that read:
"Your popularity among friends
Will bring you future success"
I kept it because I was popular
Fame never brought me success!
It caused pain and many failures.
Harsh work and persistence,
Brought me to success.
Now! I am anti-social, writing poetry
Lying fortune cookies!
Blame the Chinese

Humor

If you have a joke,
Then talk.
If you don't, then walk.
Complaints and world news?
We need no more.
Bring us humor,
Tell us a joke!

Nimir *

While bleeding, suffering from cancer
Every time I left my room door open
She'd hide in my clothes and sleep
Since she bled, Nimir never slept on my tummy
She was missing my smell
So she hid in my clothes.
Humans are not prone to such affections!

* The poet's female cat who passed away on July 23, 2002

***

Mo

I miss you, Mo
I miss walking with you.
Since the sad events,
and the political arguments.
We've not talked,
phoned each other or walked.
It is sad that we don't apologize,
Turn a new page and move on!

***

The Bath

I used to sing whenever I took a bath
When tiles began to fall, I was full of wrath
The view of broken tiles ruined my singing appetite
Turned the bathroom into a messy sight
Every time I approached contractors
They'd give me an estimate, then disappear.
Contractors are tougher to find than husbands!

End of Short Thoughts

Not A Recommended Mix

Everywhere in the world,
The "liberal" and the "conservative"
Love is a source of pain.
Love and marriage rarely have chemistry.
They are not a recommended mix.
One makes the heart over beat,
The other under beat.
One makes one insecure,
The other, if things are fine, gives you security.
Marriage deals with our physicality.
Love teases our soul with rage and tranquility.
Opposites are a healthy mix. They attract.
But not love and marriage!
Strangely one cancels the other.

Untamed Nostalgia

I am ready to rid myself of all possessions
My books and music records? Who cares!
My home? I sold it
The business? I dissolved it
The jobs? I stopped working
The car? I'll sell it.
My clothes? I can donate some and take the rest
My gold? Was given to me, I'll return it.

I'll rid myself from all possessions,
Just to be in that holy land.
In a remote village away from "civilization"
Hidden in the palm trees.
If men think I am independent and unsuitable,
The palm trees won't.
The birds and kind animals won't.
If women think I am vulgar and a threat,
Mother Nature won't.

In my conscience, was that crystal clear water.
Vivid colors underneath,
So bright in the Marshes,
All have been carved in my conscience,
And shouts: Come to us come.
They shout at me even in my dreams.
Like a nightmare,
It won't stop unless I wake up there!
I feel as if I am running out of Oxygen
What a pity if it happens before I go
No other land has contributed as much
Collect me; fold me, like a bunch
Insert me in a bag and send me home

Don't mess up with me.
I lost my mind.
How can I not when Marshes have dried up?
When millions of people have been killed,
When birds emigrated,
When thousands of ancient ruins were stolen,
When women are forced to hide their bodies?
How can I not go mad when women have been raped?
Then beaten after being raped,
When children suffer and die,
When animals are neglected,
When waters get contaminated,
When air becomes poisoned with Uranium,
When water and fish make no aquarium?
How can I not lose my mind when fear dominates?
When the land's gold and oil have been robbed?

The Nightmare does not leave me alone
All the rivers and lakes shout at me:
Come home or you'll run out of Oxygen.
I wake up with tears on my cheeks,
Untamed nostalgia has raped my soul.

About the Author

Wafaa' Al-Natheema has been writing poetry and prose since the age of nine. This is her first published book of poems. She was born and raised in Baghdad, Iraq and came to the United States in 1980. She earned bachelor degrees in civil engineering (1986), and political science (1991) and went on to work in both fields sometimes simultaneoulsy. Al-Natheema has twelve years of experience in translation from and to Arabic in the fields of Medicine, law, business and literature. She is the founder of the Institute of Near Eastern & African Studies (INEAS), a non-profit organization in Cambridge, MA.